Scriptural Rosary:
How to Pray the Rosary
and Meditate on the Mysteries

including Bible Verses, Art, Reflections, and the Fatima Story

—〰—

Kathryn Marcellino, OCDS

Abundant Life Publishing

Scriptural Rosary: How to Pray the Rosary and Meditate on the Mysteries
including Bible Verses, Art, Reflections, and the Fatima Story

by Kathryn Marcellino, OCDS

Abundant Life Publishing
PO Box 3753, Modesto, CA 95352
email: kathryn@abundantlifepublishing.com
www.AbundantLifePublishing.com
13-digit ISBN: 978-1-944158-04-0
Printed in the U.S.A.

About the Author: Kathryn Marcellino is an author, graphic designer, and the mother of five children and a number of grandchildren. She is a member of the Secular Order of Discalced Carmelites (OCDS) with a graduate certificate in Formation in Spiritual Theology from the Avila Institute. She is also a trained spiritual director with a website at www.CatholicSpiritualDirection.org where she offers an e-mail newsletter and an online course entitled "Seeking Union with God".

Kathryn Marcellino's other books include:
How to Pray the Rosary as a Pathway to Contemplation…
Twenty Mysteries of the Rosary Coloring Book…
Christian Cathedrals Stained Glass Coloring Book…
Jesse Tree Ornaments: Advent Coloring Activities and Craft Projects…
Saint Quotes on Love Catholic Meditations Coloring Book…
Art Extensions Christian Art Masterpieces Drawing and Coloring Book…
Scriptural Rosary in the Holy Land by Kathryn Marcellino and Susan Sperry

Table of Contents

—◊—

Why Pray? 4

The Rosary, the Gospel in Miniature...4

The Prayers of the Rosary are Biblical 5

Meditating on the Mysteries 5

Preparation for Prayer..5

Prayers of the Rosary...6

How to Pray the Rosary...7

Praying the Rosary...7

The 20 Mysteries of the Rosary with Scripture, Art and Reflections

1st Joyful Mystery: The Annunciation 8

2nd Joyful Mystery: The Visitation 9

3rd Joyful Mystery: The Nativity 10

4th Joyful Mystery: The Presentation in the Temple 11

5th Joyful Mystery: The Finding of Jesus in the Temple..................... 12

1st Luminous Mystery: The Baptism of the Lord 13

2nd Luminous Mystery: The Wedding Feast at Cana 14

3rd Luminous Mystery: The Proclamation of the Kingdom 15

4th Luminous Mystery: The Transfiguration 16

5th Luminous Mystery: The Institution of the Eucharist 17

1st Sorrowful Mystery: The Agony in the Garden 18

2nd Sorrowful Mystery: The Scourging at the Pillar 19

3rd Sorrowful Mystery: The Crowning with Thorns 20

4th Sorrowful Mystery: The Carrying of the Cross 21

5th Sorrowful Mystery: The Crucifixion.. 22

1st Glorious Mystery: The Resurrection 23

2nd Glorious Mystery: The Ascension.. 24

3rd Glorious Mystery: The Descent of the Holy Spirit 25

4th Glorious Mystery: The Assumption of Mary................................ 26

5th Glorious Mystery: The Coronation of Mary 27

An Overview of God's Revelation 28

The Fatima Story 30

Ideas for Praying the Family Rosary with Children 34

Fifteen Promises of the Blessed Virgin to Christians Who Faithfully Pray
the Rosary 35

Why Pray?

God is love. He created us out of love and for love. He is all good, all powerful, all knowing, and deserving of all our love. He desires our ultimate good and the good of all the universe. He is our ultimate good, happiness, and fulfillment.

"Man is placed above all creatures, and not beneath them, and he cannot be satisfied or content except in something greater than himself. Greater than himself there is nothing but Myself, the Eternal God. Therefore I alone can satisfy him" (*The Dialogue of St. Catherine of Siena, Modern English Edition*, p. 111).

Our Creator desires and commands us to love and honor him above all things as is right and just, and to love others as we love ourselves. He gives us a choice to be united to him and receive his grace, which is a sharing of his life within us.

We receive God's grace through the sacraments and prayer. Prayer is the pathway to union with God and helps us grow closer to God. It makes us better people and helps us gain inner peace. We obtain all good things that we ask for in prayer that are in accord with God's will. Jesus said, "Ask, and it shall be given you" (Matthew 7:7).

St. Alphonsus Liguori reminds us that prayer is also necessary for salvation, and that without prayer, we cannot resist temptation and keep the commandments. The Bible teaches us that without God we can do nothing good, but with him and his grace we can do all things. Jesus said, "I am the vine, you are the branches. He who abides in me and I in him, he it is that bears much fruit, for apart from me you can do nothing" (John 15:5). St. Paul said, "I can do all things in him who strengthens me" (Phil. 4:13).

The types of prayer include *adoration* (praising God), *contrition* (sorrow for sins), *petition* (asking for things and help) and *thanksgiving* (giving thanks).

Prayer is lifting our mind and heart to God. It can be as simple as speaking to God as we would to a friend as in a conversation. It can be saying vocal prayers as in the Our Father. It can be meditating (pondering) the word of God in Scripture, such as Lectio Divina. It can be praying the Rosary as Mary asked in her many apparitions.

At Fatima, Portugal, in 1917, Mary appeared to three children and asked them to, "Pray the rosary every day." One of the seers, Lucia, when asked about the importance of the Rosary said, "My impression is that the Rosary is of greatest value not only according to the words of Our Lady at Fatima, but according to the effects of the Rosary one sees throughout history. My impression is that Our Lady wanted to give ordinary people, who might not know how to pray, this simple method of getting closer to God" (www.rosary-center.org/fatimams.htm).

This book is meant to be a help to pray the Rosary as our Blessed Mother Mary taught the children at Fatima, as a form of meditation and a pathway to contemplation.

The Rosary, the Gospel in Miniature

The Rosary is sometimes called the Gospel in miniature because the mysteries cover many of the main events in the lives of Jesus Christ and his mother Mary. Most of the mysteries of the rosary are taken directly from the Gospels, which are the first four books of the New Testament. By thinking about the mysteries, we are meditating on some of the most important actions and messages of Christ in the Gospels.

The Prayers of the Rosary are Biblical

The Rosary is a Bible-based prayer. The Rosary begins with the Apostles' Creed, which is a "faithful summary of the apostles' faith" (*Catechism of the Catholic Church* #194). The Our Father is the prayer Jesus taught in Matthew 6:5-13. The Hail Mary comes mainly from Scripture and begins with the words of the Angel Gabriel's announcement to Mary that she was chosen to be the mother of Jesus the Messiah. "Hail, full of grace, the Lord is with you!" (Luke 1:28). The second sentence of the Hail Mary is from Mary's cousin Elizabeth, who exclaimed to Mary, "Blessed are you among women, and blessed is the fruit of your womb!" (Luke 1:41-42).

The idea of honoring Mary is seen in the Gospel of Luke 1:46-48, "And Mary said, 'My soul magnifies the Lord, and my spirit rejoices in God my Savior, for he has regarded the low estate of his handmaiden. For behold, henceforth all generations will call me blessed…" Jesus loves and honors his mother, and we should as well.

Meditating on the Mysteries

The rosary is prayed by saying vocal prayers while meditating on the mysteries, which helps us to better know and love Jesus and Mary. Even children can learn to pray the rosary and raise their minds and hearts to God. Our Lady of Fatima taught seven-year-old Jacinta how to meditate on the mysteries of the rosary by forming images of the mysteries in her mind as she prayed the Hail Marys.

To meditate means to think about or ponder. The *Catechism of the Catholic Church (CCC)* #2708 says, "Meditation engages thought, imagination, emotion, and desire. This mobilization of faculties is necessary in order to deepen our convictions of faith, prompt the conversion of our heart, and strengthen our will to follow Christ. Christian prayer tries above all to meditate on the mysteries of Christ, as in *Lectio Divina* or the rosary. This form of prayerful reflection is of great value, but Christian prayer should go further: to the knowledge of the love of the Lord Jesus, to union with him."

While saying the vocal prayers of the rosary, we can think about and meditate on the mystery for each decade. The Joyful Mysteries are about Jesus's conception, birth, and childhood and are said on Mondays and Saturdays. The Luminous Mysteries are about Jesus's public ministry and are said on Thursdays. The Sorrowful Mysteries are about Jesus's suffering and death and are said on Tuesdays and Fridays. The Glorious Mysteries are about events after Jesus's death and are said on Sundays and Wednesdays. (Exceptions are that the Joyful Mysteries are said on the Sundays of the Christmas Season and the Sorrowful Mysteries are said on the Sundays of Lent.)

Preparation for Prayer

Prayer is a communication between God and us. In preparation for prayer, choose a time and place for minimal outer distractions. Try to set aside all other concerns or make them part of your prayer by placing them all in God's hands. Take a moment to recollect yourself, calling to mind that you are in the presence of God, who knows and sees all and is present everywhere including within you by his grace. "Do you not know that you are God's temple and that God's Spirit dwells in you?" (1 Corinthians 3:16).

Prayers of the Rosary

—∽—

Sign of the Cross

In the name of the Father, and of the Son, and of the Holy Spirit. Amen.

Apostles' Creed

I believe in God the Father almighty, Creator of heaven and earth. And in Jesus Christ, His only Son, our Lord, who was conceived by the Holy Spirit, born of the Virgin Mary, suffered under Pontius Pilate, was crucified, died and was buried. He descended into hell; on the third day He rose again from the dead; He ascended into heaven, and sits at the right hand of God the Father almighty; from thence He will come to judge the living and the dead. I believe in the Holy Spirit, the holy Catholic Church, the communion of saints, the forgiveness of sins, the resurrection of the body and life everlasting. Amen.

Our Father

Our Father, who art in heaven, hallowed be Thy name. Thy kingdom come. Thy will be done on earth as it is in heaven. Give us this day our daily bread, and forgive us our trespasses, as we forgive those who trespass against us, and lead us not into temptation, but deliver us from evil. Amen.

Hail Mary

Hail, Mary, full of grace, the Lord is with thee. Blessed art thou amongst women and blessed is the fruit of thy womb, Jesus. Holy Mary, Mother of God, pray for us sinners, now and at the hour of our death. Amen.

Glory Be

Glory be to the Father, the Son, and the Holy Spirit; as it was in the beginning, is now, and ever shall be, world without end. Amen.

Optional Fatima Prayer

Oh my Jesus, forgive us our sins, save us from the fires of hell; lead all souls to heaven, especially those most in need of Thy Mercy.

Hail Holy Queen (Salve Regina)

Hail, Holy Queen, Mother of Mercy, our life, our sweetness, and our hope. To thee do we cry, poor banished children of Eve; to thee do we send up our sighs, mourning and weeping in this valley of tears. Turn, then, most gracious Advocate, thine eyes of mercy toward us; and after this, our exile, show unto us the blessed fruit of thy womb, Jesus. O clement, O loving, O sweet Virgin Mary.

Ending Prayers

Pray for us, O holy Mother of God. That we may be made worthy of the promises of Christ.

Let us pray. O God, whose only begotten Son, by his life, death, and resurrection, has purchased for us the rewards of eternal life, grant, we beseech Thee, that meditating upon these mysteries of the most holy Rosary of the Blessed Virgin Mary, we may imitate what they contain and obtain what they promise, through the same Christ Our Lord. Amen.

"Those who say the Rosary frequently and fervently will gradually grow in grace and holiness and will enjoy the special protection of Our Lady and the abiding friendship of God." ~ *Bishop Hugh Boyle*

How to Pray the Rosary

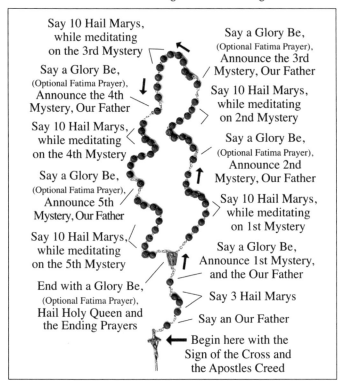

Say 10 Hail Marys, while meditating on the 3rd Mystery

Say a Glory Be, (Optional Fatima Prayer), Announce the 4th Mystery, Our Father

Say 10 Hail Marys, while meditating on the 4th Mystery

Say a Glory Be, (Optional Fatima Prayer), Announce 5th Mystery, Our Father

Say 10 Hail Marys, while meditating on the 5th Mystery

End with a Glory Be, (Optional Fatima Prayer), Hail Holy Queen and the Ending Prayers

Say a Glory Be, (Optional Fatima Prayer), Announce the 3rd Mystery, Our Father

Say 10 Hail Marys, while meditating on 2nd Mystery

Say a Glory Be, (Optional Fatima Prayer), Announce 2nd Mystery, Our Father

Say 10 Hail Marys, while meditating on 1st Mystery

Say a Glory Be, Announce 1st Mystery, and the Our Father

Say 3 Hail Marys

Say an Our Father

Begin here with the Sign of the Cross and the Apostles Creed

Praying the Rosary

One way to pray the rosary is to say the beginning six prayers of the rosary while paying attention to the meaning of the words. We begin the rosary by praying the Apostles' Creed, which contains the basic truths of the faith. Then we pray the Our Father, which is the prayer Jesus taught his disciples. Then we pray three Hail Marys asking Mary to pray for us and/or for the virtues of faith, hope, and charity. We then pray the Glory Be, a prayer of praise to God. Next we announce the first mystery, for example, "The First Joyful Mystery is The Annunciation." At this time we change our focus from thinking about the meaning of the words of the prayers to pondering the meaning of the mystery for that decade. So while we say the Our Father, 10 Hail Marys, and Glory Be for the decade, we meditate on the mystery just announced.

Ways to meditate on the mysteries include imaging oneself as present at the event. What did Jesus and Mary do and say? What might they have felt? What would I think and feel if I were one of the witnesses or participants? What does God wish to communicate to me? Does something in particular stand out to me? God enlightens us in prayer as we open our hearts and minds to him.

The following pages have art masterpieces, a Bible passage and/or other writings for each mystery, and a short reflection.

❧ THE 20 MYSTERIES OF THE ROSARY ❧

1st Joyful Mystery: The Annunciation

The Annunciation by Nicolas Poussin, 1657

Jesus Christ is the Son of God, the second Person of the Trinity, through whom all things were made (John 1). Jesus was born of the Virgin Mary, fully human while remaining fully God. Mary was a holy, young, Jewish woman. When she was a teenager and engaged to St. Joseph, the Angel Gabriel appeared to her and said, "Hail Mary, full of grace the Lord is with you." The angel told her that she was highly favored; God had chosen her to be the mother of the Messiah. He also said that this would happen through the Holy Spirit. The angel told her to name her son, "Jesus", meaning Savior. Mary said, "Behold, I am handmaid of the Lord. Let it be to me according to your word."

Luke 1:26-38 ²⁶In the sixth month the angel Gabriel was sent from God to a city of Galilee named Nazareth, ²⁷to a virgin betrothed to a man whose name was Joseph, of the house of David; and the virgin's name was Mary. ²⁸And he came to her and said, "Hail, full of grace, the Lord is with you!" ²⁹But she was greatly troubled at the saying, and considered in her mind what sort of greeting this might be. ³⁰And the angel said to her, "Do not be afraid, Mary, for you have found favor with God. ³¹And behold, you will conceive in your womb and bear a son, and you shall call his name Jesus. ³²He will be great, and will be called the Son of the Most High; and the Lord God will give to him the throne of his father David, ³³and he will reign over the house of Jacob forever; and of his kingdom there will be no end." ³⁴And Mary said to the angel, "How shall this be, since I have no husband?" ³⁵And the angel said to her, "The Holy Spirit will come upon you, and the power of the Most High will overshadow you; therefore the child to be born will be called holy, the Son of God. ³⁶And behold, your kinswoman Elizabeth in her old age has also conceived a son; and this is the sixth month with her who was called barren. ³⁷For with God nothing will be impossible." ³⁸And Mary said, "Behold, I am the handmaid of the Lord; let it be to me according to your word."

Reflection: What faith and love Mary showed God in her answer to the angel. Her trust in God's goodness for his people did not require her to understand how it might be accomplished, but only that his will be done. In what ways are you able to trust in the wisdom of God when the outcome is uncertain and things seem impossible?

When the Angel Gabriel appeared to Mary, he told her that her relative, Elizabeth (who was elderly and past child-bearing age) was going to have a baby soon. Her baby was a special person who would be called John the Baptist, and he would help prepare people for the coming of Christ. Mary went to visit Elizabeth. When Mary arrived at Elizabeth's home, Elizabeth told her that the baby John, inside her womb, leapt for joy at the presence of Jesus in Mary's womb. Elizabeth said to Mary, "Blessed are you among women, and blessed is the fruit of your womb," which is the second sentence of the Hail Mary prayer.

Visitation by Domenico Ghirlandaio, 1491

Luke 1:39-49, 57-60 ³⁹ In those days Mary arose and went with haste into the hill country, to a city of Judah, ⁴⁰ and she entered the house of Zechariah and greeted Elizabeth. ⁴¹ And when Elizabeth heard the greeting of Mary, the babe leaped in her womb; and Elizabeth was filled with the Holy Spirit ⁴² and she exclaimed with a loud cry, "Blessed are you among women, and blessed is the fruit of your womb! ⁴³ And why is this granted me that the mother of my Lord should come to me? ⁴⁴ For behold, when the voice of your greeting came to my ears, the babe in my womb leaped for joy. ⁴⁵ And blessed is she who believed that there would be a fulfillment of what was spoken to her from the Lord." ⁴⁶ And Mary said, "My soul magnifies the Lord, ⁴⁷ and my spirit rejoices in God my Savior, ⁴⁸ for he has regarded the low estate of his handmaiden. For behold, henceforth all generations will call me blessed; ⁴⁹ for he who is mighty has done great things for me, and holy is his name...." ⁵⁶ And Mary remained with her about three months, and returned to her home. ⁵⁷ Now the time came for Elizabeth to be delivered, and she gave birth to a son. ⁵⁸ And her neighbors and kinsfolk heard that the Lord had shown great mercy to her, and they rejoiced with her. ⁵⁹ And on the eighth day they came to circumcise the child; and they would have named him Zechariah after his father, ⁶⁰ but his mother said, "Not so; he shall be called John."

Reflection: Mary loved God above all things and others as she loved herself. This mystery shows the joy of both giving and receiving. As Mary was given the great gift of knowing how God had honored her, her thoughts turned to how she could help and honor her relative, Elizabeth. In journeying to humbly assist her, she was received with joy and honor herself. It is in giving unselfishly that we, in return, receive. When it is inconvenient or cumbersome, how often do we humbly seek to help others?

The Nativity by Lorenzo Lotto, 1523

When it was almost time for Jesus to be born, Mary and Joseph, her husband, were required by law to travel to Bethlehem for a census. When they arrived, there were no rooms left for them so they stayed in a stable or cave for animals. While there, Mary's time came. She gave birth to Baby Jesus and laid him in a manger. We call the day Jesus was born, Christmas. At the time Jesus was born, angels appeared to shepherds in the field nearby who were taking care of their sheep. The angels sang praises to God and told the shepherds that a Savior had been born, who is Christ the Lord. The shepherds hurried to see Baby Jesus and found him lying in a manger.

Luke 2:1, 3-16 [1]In those days a decree went out from Caesar Augustus that all the world should be enrolled.... [3]And all went to be enrolled, each to his own city. [4]And Joseph also went up from Galilee, from the city of Nazareth, to Judea, to the city of David, which is called Bethlehem, because he was of the house and lineage of David, [5]to be enrolled with Mary, his betrothed, who was with child. [6]And while they were there, the time came for her to be delivered. [7]And she gave birth to her first-born son and wrapped him in swaddling clothes, and laid him in a manger, because there was no place for them in the inn. [8]And in that region there were shepherds out in the field, keeping watch over their flock by night. [9]And an angel of the Lord appeared to them, and the glory of the Lord shone around them, and they were filled with fear. [10]And the angel said to them, "Be not afraid; for behold, I bring you good news of a great joy which will come to all the people; [11]for to you is born this day in the city of David a Savior, who is Christ the Lord. [12]And this will be a sign for you: you will find a babe wrapped in swaddling clothes and lying in a manger." [13]And suddenly there was with the angel a multitude of the heavenly host praising God and saying, [14]"Glory to God in the highest, and on earth peace among men with whom he is pleased!" [15]When the angels went away from them into heaven, the shepherds said to one another, "Let us go over to Bethlehem and see this thing that has happened, which the Lord has made known to us." [16]And they went with haste, and found Mary and Joseph, and the babe lying in a manger.

Reflection: Jesus, while remaining the Son of God, was born a human being. He said he would be with us always, even until the end of the world. How can we love Jesus today?

Forty days after Jesus was born, Joseph and Mary took Jesus to the Temple in Jerusalem for Mary's ritual purification after childbirth and to present Jesus as firstborn in obedience to the Law of Moses. While they were there, the Holy Spirit informed the devout Simeon that Jesus was the Messiah. Simeon took Jesus in his arms and gave praise and thanks to God for allowing him to see the Messiah. Simeon told Mary that her child was set for the falling and rising of many in Israel, and that she would have much to suffer. Anna, an elderly prophetess, was also in the Temple offering prayers and thanks to God for Jesus. She told everyone there about Jesus.

Presentation in the Temple
by Giotto di Bondone, 1304-1306

Luke 2:22-33 [22] And when the time came for their purification according to the law of Moses, they brought him up to Jerusalem to present him to the Lord [23] (as it is written in the law of the Lord, "Every male that opens the womb shall be called holy to the Lord") [24] and to offer a sacrifice according to what is said in the law of the Lord, "a pair of turtledoves, or two young pigeons." [25] Now there was a man in Jerusalem, whose name was Simeon, and this man was righteous and devout, looking for the consolation of Israel, and the Holy Spirit was upon him. [26] And it had been revealed to him by the Holy Spirit that he should not see death before he had seen the Lord's Christ. [27] And inspired by the Spirit he came into the temple; and when the parents brought in the child Jesus, to do for him according to the custom of the law, [28] he took him up in his arms and blessed God and said, [29] "Lord, now lettest thou thy servant depart in peace, according to thy word; [30] for mine eyes have seen thy salvation [31] which thou hast prepared in the presence of all peoples, [32] a light for revelation to the Gentiles, and for glory to thy people Israel." [33] And his father and his mother marveled at what was said about him.

Reflection: Jesus, Mary, and Joseph obeyed the laws of Moses in effect at their time. The Bible says, "Let every person be subject to the governing authorities. For there is no authority except from God, and those that exist have been instituted by God. Therefore he who resists the authorities resists what God has appointed, and those who resist will incur judgment" (Romans 13:1-2). However, "If rulers were to enact unjust laws or take measures contrary to the moral order, such arrangements would not be binding in conscience." (*CCC* 1903) Do you obey the just laws of authorities over you?

Finding in the Temple, Austria

When Jesus was 12 years old, he went with his parents to Jerusalem to celebrate the feast of the Passover. On the way back home, Mary and his step-father, Joseph, couldn't find Jesus among their relatives and friends. They looked for him for three days and finally found him in the Temple talking to the teachers who were amazed at how much Jesus knew about God and the things pertaining to God. Mary and Joseph asked Jesus why he had stayed behind without telling them, as they had been worried about him. He said to them, "Did you not know that I must be in my Father's house?" His parents didn't understand what he meant. Even though Jesus was the Son of God, he returned home with his parents and was obedient to them. His mother Mary thought about all these things and kept them in her heart.

Luke 2:40-51   [40] And the child grew and became strong, filled with wisdom; and the favor of God was upon him. [41] Now his parents went to Jerusalem every year at the feast of the Passover. [42] And when he was twelve years old, they went up according to custom; [43] and when the feast was ended, as they were returning, the boy Jesus stayed behind in Jerusalem. His parents did not know it, [44] but supposing him to be in the company they went a day's journey, and they sought him among their kinsfolk and acquaintances; [45] and when they did not find him, they returned to Jerusalem, seeking him. [46] After three days they found him in the temple, sitting among the teachers, listening to them and asking them questions; [47] and all who heard him were amazed at his understanding and his answers. [48] And when they saw him they were astonished; and his mother said to him, "Son, why have you treated us so? Behold, your father and I have been looking for you anxiously." [49] And he said to them, "How is it that you sought me? Did you not know that I must be in my Father's house?" [50] And they did not understand the saying which he spoke to them. [51] And he went down with them and came to Nazareth, and was obedient to them; and his mother kept all these things in her heart.

Reflection: When Jesus talks about his Father's house, he is speaking of his Father in heaven. Jesus calls us to become God's children and to call God our Father. "Our justification comes from the grace of God. Grace is *favor*, the free and undeserved help that God gives us to respond to his call to become children of God, adoptive sons, partakers of the divine nature and of eternal life" (*Catechism of the Catholic Church* #1996). Even as a child, Jesus answered his Heavenly Father's call to teach people about God. Are you responding to God's commandments and callings in your life?

When Jesus grew up, it was time for him to leave his parents' home and teach the people. John the Baptist had had gone before Jesus and preached a "baptism of repentance for the forgiveness of sins". John called people to repent, which means to be sorry for their sins, and to stop sinning. John told the people he was not the Christ, but his mission was to get things ready for the coming of Christ. When Jesus went down to the Jordan River, he asked John to baptize him. When John baptized Jesus, the heavens opened up and the Holy Spirit descended upon Jesus like a dove. A voice from heaven said, "Thou art my beloved Son; with thee I am well pleased."

The Baptism of Christ
by Bartolomé Esteban Murillo, 1655

 Mark 1: 1-5, 7-11

[1]The beginning of the gospel of Jesus Christ, the Son of God. [2]As it is written in Isaiah the prophet, "Behold, I send my messenger before thy face, who shall prepare thy way; [3]the voice of one crying in the wilderness: Prepare the way of the Lord, make his paths straight." [4]John the baptizer appeared in the wilderness, preaching a baptism of repentance for the forgiveness of sins. [5]And there went out to him all the country of Judea, and all the people of Jerusalem; and they were baptized by him in the river Jordan, confessing their sins.... [7]And he preached, saying, "After me comes he who is mightier than I, the thong of whose sandals I am not worthy to stoop down and untie. [8]I have baptized you with water; but he will baptize you with the Holy Spirit." [9]In those days Jesus came from Nazareth of Galilee and was baptized by John in the Jordan. [10]And when he came up out of the water, immediately he saw the heavens opened and the Spirit descending upon him like a dove; [11]and a voice came from heaven, "Thou art my beloved Son; with thee I am well pleased."

> **Reflection:** Jesus was baptized and said we need to be born again, which happens in the sacrament of baptism. Jesus said, "Truly, truly, I say to you, unless one is born of water and the Spirit, he cannot enter the kingdom of God" (John 3:5). "And Peter said…'Repent, and be baptized every one of you in the name of Jesus Christ for the forgiveness of your sins; and you shall receive the gift of the Holy Spirit'" (Acts: 2-38). God offers us sanctifying grace in baptism. Do you desire to be baptized if you haven't been already?

A 14th century fresco from the Visoki Dečani monastery in Metohia (Kosovo)

Jesus, his mother, and his disciples were attending a wedding when the party ran out of wine. Jesus's mother, Mary, told Jesus, "They have no wine." Even though Jesus said it was not yet time to reveal his power to the world, Mary told the servants, "Do whatever he tells you" (John 2:5). Jesus ordered the servants to fill the big stone jars with water and to take some of it to the head waiter. After tasting it, the head waiter congratulated the bridegroom on saving the best wine for last. This was the first miracle or sign Jesus did that revealed Jesus's glory as the Son of God; and his disciples believed in him. Jesus performed many other miracles later.

 John 2: 1-11

[1] On the third day there was a marriage at Cana in Galilee, and the mother of Jesus was there; [2] Jesus also was invited to the marriage, with his disciples. [3] When the wine failed, the mother of Jesus said to him, "They have no wine." [4] And Jesus said to her, "O woman, what have you to do with me? My hour has not yet come." [5] His mother said to the servants, "Do whatever he tells you." [6] Now six stone jars were standing there, for the Jewish rites of purification, each holding twenty or thirty gallons. [7] Jesus said to them, "Fill the jars with water." And they filled them up to the brim, [8] He said to them, "Now draw some out, and take it to the steward of the feast." So they took it. [9] When the steward of the feast tasted the water now become wine, and did not know where it came from (though the servants who had drawn the water knew), the steward of the feast called the bridegroom [10] and said to him, "Every man serves the good wine first; and when men have drunk freely, then the poor wine; but you have kept the good wine until now." [11] This, the first of his signs, Jesus did at Cana in Galilee, and manifested his glory; and his disciples believed in him.

Reflection: Jesus showed that he was God by performing miracles. Mary did not tell Jesus what to do. She rather told him the problem and put it his hands to take care of. This is a good practice for us to follow as God knows best. Do you do whatever God tells you and pray for acceptance of God's way of doing things? Are you patient while waiting for God to answer your prayers realizing that God's plan and timing is best?

When Jesus was about 30 years old, he went out to teach the people and proclaim the Gospel. (Gospel means "good news.") The good news is that the kingdom of God was at hand. Jesus said to believe in God and ask for the forgiveness of sins. Jesus taught people what God wanted them to do and how they should live. He told them to have faith in him, to stop sinning, to obey God's commandments, and to love God and their neighbor. He worked miracles to show people that he was God, including healing the sick and raising the dead.

The Sermon on the Mount by Carl Heinrich Bloch

Mark 1:15 15 and saying, "The time is fulfilled, and the kingdom of God is at hand; repent, and believe in the gospel.

Mark 2: 3-12 3And they came, bringing to him a paralytic carried by four men. 4And when they could not get near him because of the crowd, they removed the roof above him; and when they had made an opening, they let down the pallet on which the paralytic lay. 5And when Jesus saw their faith, he said to the paralytic, "My son, your sins are forgiven." 6Now some of the scribes were sitting there, questioning in their hearts, 7"Why does this man speak thus? It is blasphemy! Who can forgive sins but God alone?" 8And immediately Jesus, perceiving in his spirit that they thus questioned within themselves, said to them, "Why do you question thus in your hearts? 9Which is easier, to say to the paralytic, 'Your sins are forgiven,' or to say, 'Rise, take up your pallet and walk?' 10But that you may know that the Son of man has authority on earth to forgive sins," he said to the paralytic, 11"I say to you, rise, take up your pallet and go home." 12And he rose, and immediately took up the pallet and went out before them all; so that they were all amazed and glorified God, saying, "We never saw anything like this!"

Luke 7:47-48 47Therefore I tell you, her sins, which are many, are forgiven, for she loved much; but he who is forgiven little, loves little." 48 And he said to her, "Your sins are forgiven."

John 20:22-23 22And when he had said this, he breathed on them, and said to them, "Receive the Holy Spirit. 23 If you forgive the sins of any, they are forgiven; if you retain the sins of any, they are retained."

Reflection: We need to study, especially the Bible and the teachings of the Church such as the *Catechism of the Catholic Church* (www.vatican.va) to know and understand what God requires of us. We also need to believe in Jesus and obey him to be in the kingdom of God. Do you study the teachings of Jesus and do what he asks of you?

The Transfiguration by Raphael, 1516-1520

Jesus went up a high mountain with Peter, James, and John. While they were there, he was changed so that his face shone like the sun and his clothes became as white as light. The apostles with him saw Moses and Elijah talking to him. From a bright cloud a voice said, "This is my beloved Son, with whom I am well pleased, listen to him" (Matthew 7:5). The apostles were filled with awe and fell down on the ground. When they looked up again they only saw Jesus there. On the way back down the mountain, Jesus told the three apostles not to tell anyone what they had seen until he had risen from the dead. This was God's way to show the apostles they should listen to Jesus, his Son, who is above even the Law of Moses and the prophets like Elijah.

Matthew 17:1-9 ¹And after six days Jesus took with him Peter and James and John his brother, and led them up a high mountain apart. ²And he was transfigured before them, and his face shone like the sun, and his garments became white as light. ³And behold, there appeared to them Moses and Elijah, talking with him. ⁴And Peter said to Jesus, "Lord, it is well that we are here; if you wish, I will make three booths here, one for you and one for Moses and one for Elijah." ⁵He was still speaking, when lo, a bright cloud overshadowed them, and a voice from the cloud said, "This is my beloved Son, with whom I am well pleased; listen to him." ⁶When the disciples heard this, they fell on their faces, and were filled with awe. ⁷But Jesus came and touched them, saying, "Rise, and have no fear." ⁸And when they lifted up their eyes, they saw no one but Jesus only. ⁹And as they were coming down the mountain, Jesus commanded them, "Tell no one the vision, until the Son of man is raised from the dead."

> **Reflection:** Jesus revealed his glory to Peter, James, and John. He allowed them to see that he was not just an ordinary human being, but the Son of God. Do you realize that Jesus is really God who became a man to save us from our sins, to give us grace, to teach us the truth, and help us to get to heaven? Do you put God first in your life?

The Last Supper by Leonardo da Vinci, 1495-1498

The night before Jesus died on the cross, he had his last supper with his apostles. It was on the Jewish feast of Passover when a lamb was slain and eaten in remembrance of God and Moses bringing the Israelites out of slavery from the land of Egypt. At Mass, Jesus is called the "Lamb of God who takes away the sins of the world" (John 1:29). In the Old Testament, animal sacrifices were offered for sins. However, the sacrifice that Jesus made by dying on the cross made up for all the sins of the entire world. After Jesus's perfect sacrifice of himself, there wasn't a need for more animal sacrifices. When Jesus said to the apostles, "Do this in remembrance of me" (Luke 22:19), he instituted the sacrament of the Eucharist also called Holy Communion. Jesus desires to be united in communion with us. He loves us and wants us to love him in return and to love one another.

Matthew 26:17-20, 26-30 ¹⁷Now on the first day of Unleavened Bread the disciples came to Jesus, saying, "Where will you have us prepare for you to eat the passover?" ¹⁸He said, "Go into the city to a certain one, and say to him, `The Teacher says, My time is at hand; I will keep the passover at your house with my disciples.'" ¹⁹And the disciples did as Jesus had directed them, and they prepared the passover. ²⁰When it was evening, he sat at table with the twelve disciples;... ²⁶Now as they were eating, Jesus took bread, and blessed, and broke it, and gave it to the disciples and said, "Take, eat; this is my body." ²⁷And he took a cup, and when he had given thanks he gave it to them, saying, "Drink of it, all of you; ²⁸for this is my blood of the covenant, which is poured out for many for the forgiveness of sins. ²⁹I tell you I shall not drink again of this fruit of the vine until that day when I drink it new with you in my Father's kingdom." ³⁰And when they had sung a hymn, they went out to the Mount of Olives.

> **Reflection:** At each Mass, the priest follows Jesus's instructions at his last supper to "Do this in remembrance of me" (Luke 22:19). At Mass during the words of consecration, the water and wine are changed into Jesus's body and blood. In Holy Communion, we receive the body, blood, soul, and divinity of Jesus Christ under the appearances of bread and wine. Isn't it wonderful to be able to receive Jesus in this special way?

Jesus praying to God the Father in Gethsemane by Heinrich Hofmann, 1890

Right after having his last supper with the apostles, Jesus went to the Garden of Gethsemane to pray. He was suffering so much that "his sweat became like great drops of blood falling upon the ground" (Luke 22:44). He was with Peter, James, and John, and he asked them to stay awake for an hour and pray. Jesus knew that he would soon be suffering greatly and dying on the cross to make up for all the sins of the world. He prayed three times to his Father in heaven to not have to suffer so much, but he wanted God the Father's will to be done and not his own will. Each time he checked on the apostles, they were asleep; and an angel came from heaven to help strengthen Jesus. Today the "holy hour" devotion comes from Jesus's request to his apostles to spend an hour with him in prayer.

Matthew 26:36-46 ³⁶Then Jesus went with them to a place called Gethsemane, and he said to his disciples, "Sit here, while I go yonder and pray." ³⁷And taking with him Peter and the two sons of Zebedee, he began to be sorrowful and troubled. ³⁸Then he said to them, "My soul is very sorrowful, even to death; remain here, and watch with me." ³⁹And going a little farther he fell on his face and prayed, "My Father, if it be possible, let this cup pass from me; nevertheless, not as I will, but as thou wilt." ⁴⁰And he came to the disciples and found them sleeping; and he said to Peter, "So, could you not watch with me one hour? ⁴¹Watch and pray that you may not enter into temptation; the spirit indeed is willing, but the flesh is weak." ⁴²Again, for the second time, he went away and prayed, "My Father, if this cannot pass unless I drink it, thy will be done." ⁴³And again he came and found them sleeping, for their eyes were heavy. ⁴⁴So, leaving them again, he went away and prayed for the third time, saying the same words. ⁴⁵Then he came to the disciples and said to them, "Are you still sleeping and taking your rest? Behold, the hour is at hand, and the Son of man is betrayed into the hands of sinners. ⁴⁶Rise, let us be going; see, my betrayer is at hand."

Reflection: Jesus suffered greatly in the Garden of Gethsemane. He saw clearly what he was about to undergo in his passion and death. He prayed, "My Father, if it be possible, let this cup pass from me; nevertheless, not as I will, but as thou wilt" (Matthew 26:39). This is a beautiful lesson on how to pray during our own suffering and to offer up our sufferings as Jesus did. "We know that in everything God works for good with those who love him, who are called according to his purpose" (Romans 8:28).

After Jesus prayed in the Garden of Gethsemane, a crowd came with swords and clubs, and arrested him. They took him to the high priest, and they asked if he was the Messiah, the Son of God. Jesus said that he was. The chief priests and elders didn't believe him and accused him of blasphemy, which means being disrespectful to God or claiming to be God. In the morning, they handed him over to the Roman ruler, Pontius Pilate. Pilate asked Jesus if he was the "King of the Jews." Jesus said that his Kingdom was not of this world. Pilate didn't want to be responsible for putting Jesus to death, so he let the crowd decide, and they shouted to crucify Jesus. Pilate had Jesus cruelly whipped.

The Scourging, illumination on parchment, circa 1503-4, unknown artist

John 18:28-40, 19:1 ²⁸Then they led Jesus from the house of Caiaphas to the praetorium. It was early. They themselves did not enter the praetorium, so that they might not be defiled, but might eat the passover. ²⁹So Pilate went out to them and said, "What accusation do you bring against this man?" ³⁰They answered him, "If this man were not an evildoer, we would not have handed him over." ³¹Pilate said to them, "Take him yourselves and judge him by your own law." The Jews said to him, "It is not lawful for us to put any man to death." ³²This was to fulfil the word which Jesus had spoken to show by what death he was to die. ³³Pilate entered the praetorium again and called Jesus, and said to him, "Are you the King of the Jews?" ³⁴Jesus answered, "Do you say this of your own accord, or did others say it to you about me?" ³⁵Pilate answered, "Am I a Jew? Your own nation and the chief priests have handed you over to me; what have you done?" ³⁶Jesus answered, "My kingship is not of this world; if my kingship were of this world, my servants would fight, that I might not be handed over to the Jews; but my kingship is not from the world." ³⁷Pilate said to him, "So you are a king?" Jesus answered, "You say that I am a king. For this I was born, and for this I have come into the world, to bear witness to the truth. Every one who is of the truth hears my voice." ³⁸Pilate said to him, "What is truth?" After he had said this, he went out to the Jews again, and told them, "I find no crime in him. ³⁹But you have a custom that I should release one man for you at the Passover; will you have me release for you the King of the Jews?" ⁴⁰They cried out again, "Not this man, but Barabbas!" Now Barabbas was a robber....¹⁹:¹Then Pilate took Jesus and scourged him.

Reflection: Jesus offered himself as a perfect sacrifice to make up for our sins and the sins of the world. What response should we have to Jesus's sacrifice for us?

Ecce Homo (Behold, the Man!)
by Bartolomé Esteban Murillo, circa 1675

After Jesus was whipped, scourged, and bleeding all over, they ridiculed him. They took off his clothes and put on a royal purple cloak and made a crown of thorns to put on his head. They saluted him and said, "Hail, King of the Jews!" (Matthew 27:29). They struck his head with a stick to torture him. They spat on him and knelt down to pretend to do him homage to humiliate him. Pilate brought Jesus out before the crowd again in the purple cloak and said, "Behold the Man!" (John 19:5). Pilate said that he found no fault in Jesus, but the crowd shouted, "Crucify him."

Mark 15:6-20 ⁶Now on the occasion of the feast he used to release to them one prisoner whom they requested. ⁷A man called Barabbas was then in prison along with the rebels who had committed murder in a rebellion. ⁸The crowd came forward and began to ask him to do for them as he was accustomed. ⁹Pilate answered, "Do you want me to release to you the king of the Jews?" ¹⁰For he knew that it was out of envy that the chief priests had handed him over. ¹¹But the chief priests stirred up the crowd to have him release Barabbas for them instead. ¹²Pilate again said to them in reply, "Then what [do you want] me to do with [the man you call] the king of the Jews?" ¹³They shouted again, "Crucify him." ¹⁴Pilate said to them, "Why? What evil has he done?" They only shouted the louder, "Crucify him." ¹⁵So Pilate, wishing to satisfy the crowd, released Barabbas to them and, after he had Jesus scourged, handed him over to be crucified. *Mockery by the Soldiers.* ¹⁶The soldiers led him away inside the palace, that is, the praetorium, and assembled the whole cohort. ¹⁷They clothed him in purple and, weaving a crown of thorns, placed it on him. ¹⁸They began to salute him with, "Hail, King of the Jews!" ¹⁹and kept striking his head with a reed and spitting upon him. They knelt before him in homage. ²⁰And when they had mocked him, they stripped him of the purple cloak, dressed him in his own clothes, and led him out to crucify him. *(NABRE).*

Reflection: People can be cruel. Although Jesus was ridiculed and tortured, Jesus prayed for those who hurt him. God is all good and loves everyone including sinners. Jesus said to bless those who curse you, and to return good for evil. Do you do this in your life? "Do not be overcome by evil, but overcome evil with good" (Romans 12:21).

Christ Carrying the Cross by Eustache Le Sueur, 1617-55

Jesus was led away to be crucified and made to carry his cross. At one point, the soldiers forced Simon of Cyrene to help carry the cross. People were following Jesus and some women were crying. According to tradition, one women was Veronica. She wiped Jesus's face with her veil, and a miracle took place as a picture of Jesus's face was left on her veil.

Luke 23:13-28 [13]Pilate then summoned the chief priests, the rulers, and the people [14]and said to them, "You brought this man to me and accused him of inciting the people to revolt. I have conducted my investigation in your presence and have not found this man guilty of the charges you have brought against him [15]nor did Herod, for he sent him back to us. So no capital crime has been committed by him. [16]Therefore I shall have him flogged and then release him."[17] *The Sentence of Death.* [18]But all together they shouted out, "Away with this man! Release Barabbas to us." [19](Now Barabbas had been imprisoned for a rebellion that had taken place in the city and for murder.) [20]Again Pilate addressed them, still wishing to release Jesus, [21]but they continued their shouting, "Crucify him! Crucify him!" [22]Pilate addressed them a third time, "What evil has this man done? I found him guilty of no capital crime. Therefore I shall have him flogged and then release him." [23]With loud shouts, however, they persisted in calling for his crucifixion, and their voices prevailed. [24]The verdict of Pilate was that their demand should be granted. [25]So he released the man who had been imprisoned for rebellion and murder, for whom they asked, and he handed Jesus over to them to deal with as they wished. *The Way of the Cross.* [26]As they led him away they took hold of a certain Simon, a Cyrenian, who was coming in from the country; and after laying the cross on him, they made him carry it behind Jesus. [27]A large crowd of people followed Jesus, including many women who mourned and lamented him. [28]Jesus turned to them and said, "Daughters of Jerusalem, do not weep for me; weep instead for yourselves and for your children..." *(NABRE)*

Reflection: Jesus said, "If any man would come after me, let him deny himself and take up his cross daily and follow me" (Luke 9:23). Have you decided to follow Jesus? Do you offer up your sufferings for the conversion of sinners and salvation of souls?

Crucifixion, 19th Century artist

When they arrived at Mt. Calvary, they stripped Jesus of his clothes and nailed him to the cross. Jesus was offered wine mixed with gall to drink. He was then crucified between two thieves. According to Mark's Gospel, Jesus hung on the cross for about six hours from nine in the morning until his death at about three in the afternoon. The soldiers put a sign on the cross above his head, which said, "Jesus of Nazareth, King of the Jews" (John 19:20). They divided his garments and cast lots for his robe. The soldiers didn't break Jesus's legs, as they did to the other two men crucified by him. A soldier thrust a lance into his side, and blood and water flowed out showing that Jesus was dead. Then they buried him.

 ## Luke 23:33, 35-49

[33]And when they came to the place which is called The Skull, there they crucified him, and the criminals, one on the right and one on the left. [35]And the people stood by, watching; but the rulers scoffed at him, saying, "He saved others; let him save himself, if he is the Christ of God, his Chosen One!" [36]The soldiers also mocked him, coming up and offering him vinegar, [37]and saying, "If you are the King of the Jews, save yourself!" [38]There was also an inscription over him, "This is the King of the Jews." [39]One of the criminals who were hanged railed at him, saying, "Are you not the Christ? Save yourself and us!" [40]But the other rebuked him, saying, "Do you not fear God, since you are under the same sentence of condemnation? [41]And we indeed justly; for we are receiving the due reward of our deeds; but this man has done nothing wrong." [42]And he said, "Jesus, remember me when you come into your kingdom." [43]And he said to him, "Truly, I say to you, today you will be with me in Paradise." [44]It was now about the sixth hour, and there was darkness over the whole land until the ninth hour, [45]while the sun's light failed; and the curtain of the temple was torn in two. [46]Then Jesus, crying with a loud voice, said, "Father, into thy hands I commit my spirit!" And having said this he breathed his last. [47]Now when the centurion saw what had taken place, he praised God, and said, "Certainly this man was innocent!" [48]And all the multitudes who assembled to see the sight, when they saw what had taken place, returned home beating their breasts. [49]And all his acquaintances and the women who had followed him from Galilee stood at a distance and saw these things.

Reflection: Jesus offered himself as a sacrifice for sin and made it possible for us to go to heaven someday. No matter how great our sins, Jesus's mercy is greater. Jesus loves us, died for us, and wants to forgive us. He is a greater Savior than we are a sinner. Jesus greatly desires that we trust in his mercy. Do you trust Jesus? (www.divinemercy.org)

📖 Matthew 28:1-10, 16-20

[1] After the sabbath, as the first day of the week was dawning, Mary Magdalene and the other Mary came to see the tomb. [2]And behold, there was a great earthquake; for an angel of the Lord descended from heaven, approached, rolled back the stone, and sat upon it.[3] His appearance was like lightning and his clothing was white as snow. [4]The guards were shaken with fear of him and became like dead men. [5]Then the angel said to the women in reply, "Do not be afraid! I know that you are seeking Jesus the crucified. [6] He is not here, for he has been raised just as he said. Come and see the place where he lay. [7] Then go quickly and tell his disciples, 'He has been raised from the dead, and he is going before you to Galilee; there you will see him.' Behold, I have told you." [8]Then they went away quickly from the tomb, fearful yet overjoyed, and ran to announce this to his disciples. [9]And behold, Jesus met them on their way and greeted them. They approached, embraced his feet, and did him homage. [10]Then Jesus said to them, "Do not be afraid. Go tell my brothers to go to Galilee, and there they will see me."…
[16] The eleven disciples went to Galilee, to the mountain to which Jesus had ordered them. [17] When they saw him, they worshiped, but they doubted. [18] Then Jesus approached and said to them, "All power in heaven and on earth has been given to me. [19] Go, therefore, and make disciples of all nations, baptizing them in the name of the Father, and of the Son, and of the holy Spirit, [20]teaching them to observe all that I have commanded you. And behold, I am with you always, until the end of the age." *(NABRE)*

Resurrection, by Carl Heinrich Bloch, 1873

After death, Jesus's body was wrapped in a linen cloth and buried. On the third day, he rose from the dead. Mary Magdalene and another Mary visited the tomb. They found the stone rolled back and Jesus's body was missing, and saw an angel. Later Jesus appeared to them and said to tell the apostles all they had seen. Jesus appeared many times to the apostles and others.

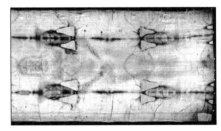

The Shroud of Turin is thought to be the burial cloth of Jesus. Many scientific studies were done on the image including one by the STURP team of American scientists. They found no reliable evidence of forgery and said it's "a mystery" of how the image was formed. (www.shroud.com)

Reflection: Jesus's body rose from the dead, and our bodies will also rise on the last day. "…and those he justified, he also glorified" (Rom. 8:30). "…For the trumpet will sound, and the dead will be raised imperishable, and we will be changed." (1 Cor. 15:52).

Ascension of Jesus, ceiling painting in parish church in Spittal an der Drau 3, Austria

One evening after Jesus rose from the dead, he appeared to the disciples and said, "Peace be with you." He showed them his hands, feet, and side. The disciples were very happy to see him. Jesus said to them, "As the Father has sent me, even so I send you." He breathed on them and said, "Receive the Holy Spirit. If you forgive the sins of any, they are forgiven; if you retain the sins of any, they are retained" (from John 20:19-23). Jesus appeared many other times and performed many other signs as well. One day, he told the apostles that they would be baptized with the Holy Spirit soon. Then Jesus was lifted up in a cloud and went to heaven. Two men with white robes told the disciples that Jesus will come again from heaven on a cloud.

Acts 1:1-11 [1]In the first book, Theophilus, I dealt with all that Jesus did and taught [2]until the day he was taken up, after giving instructions through the holy Spirit to the apostles whom he had chosen. [3]He presented himself alive to them by many proofs after he had suffered, appearing to them during forty days and speaking about the kingdom of God. [4]While meeting with them, he enjoined them not to depart from Jerusalem, but to wait for "the promise of the Father about which you have heard me speak; [5]for John baptized with water, but in a few days you will be baptized with the holy Spirit." *The Ascension of Jesus.* [6]When they had gathered together they asked him, "Lord, are you at this time going to restore the kingdom to Israel?" [7]He answered them, "It is not for you to know the times or seasons that the Father has established by his own authority. [8]But you will receive power when the holy Spirit comes upon you, and you will be my witnesses in Jerusalem, throughout Judea and Samaria, and to the ends of the earth." [9]When he had said this, as they were looking on, he was lifted up, and a cloud took him from their sight. [10]While they were looking intently at the sky as he was going, suddenly two men dressed in white garments stood beside them. [11]They said, "Men of Galilee, why are you standing there looking at the sky? This Jesus who has been taken up from you into heaven will return in the same way as you have seen him going into heaven." *(NABRE)*

Reflection: With Jesus's death, his suffering ended, and ours will too if we die in God's grace. "And when I go and prepare a place for you, I will come again and will take you to myself, that where I am you may be also" (John 14:3). "…What no eye has seen, nor ear heard, nor the heart of man conceived, what God has prepared for those who love him" (1 Cor. 2:9). Do you look forward to being with God in heaven someday?

After Jesus went up into heaven, the apostles went back to Jerusalem and spent their time in prayer. When the day of Pentecost came they were gathered in one place. All of a sudden from the sky came a loud noise like a strong wind. Tongues as of fire came to rest on each of them, and they were filled with the Holy Spirit. Many people from various places were in Jerusalem that day, and the apostles told them the good news about Jesus, the Messiah. They heard them speak in their own language and asked what to do. Peter said, "Repent and be baptized…in the name of Jesus Christ that your sins may be forgiven; then you shall receive the gift of the Holy Spirit" (Acts 2:38). About 3,000 people were baptized that day. Pentecost is often called the birthday of the Church.

Pentecost by El Greco, 1600s

Acts 2:1-8, 12 [1]When the day of Pentecost had come, they were all together in one place. [2]And suddenly a sound came from heaven like the rush of a mighty wind, and it filled all the house where they were sitting. [3]And there appeared to them tongues as of fire, distributed and resting on each one of them. [4]And they were all filled with the Holy Spirit and began to speak in other tongues, as the Spirit gave them utterance. [5]Now there were dwelling in Jerusalem, Jews, devout men from every nation under heaven. [6]And at this sound the multitude came together, and they were bewildered, because each one heard them speaking in his own language. [7]And they were amazed and wondered, saying, "Are not all these who are speaking Galileans? [8]And how is it that we hear, each of us in his own native language? …[11]…we hear them telling in our own tongues the mighty works of God." [12]And all were amazed and perplexed, saying to one another, "What does this mean?" [13]But others mocking said, "They are filled with new wine." [14]But Peter, standing with the eleven, lifted up his voice and addressed them, "Men of Judea and all who dwell in Jerusalem, let this be known to you, and give ear to my words. [15]For these men are not drunk, as you suppose, since it is only the third hour of the day; [16]but this is what was spoken by the prophet Joel: [17]'And in the last days it shall be, God declares, that I will pour out my Spirit upon all flesh, and your sons and your daughters shall prophesy, and your young men shall see visions, and your old men shall dream dreams; [18] yea, and on my menservants and my maidservants in those days I will pour out my Spirit; and they shall prophesy.'"

Reflection: "…Confirmation is the special outpouring of the Holy Spirit as once granted to the apostles on the day of Pentecost" (*CCC* #1302). The promise is for all "whom the Lord our God calls to him" (Act 2:39). Are you answering God's call?

The Assumption of the Virgin
by Bartolomé Esteban Murillo, 1670s

Mary was honored by God to be the mother of Jesus. God created her without the stain of Original Sin on her soul because she was going to be the mother of Jesus. She lived a very holy life doing all that God asked her. When it was time for Mary to die, Mary's body and soul were taken up to heaven to be with God. Based on a longstanding tradition of the church, Pius XII infallibly defined the Assumption of Mary as a dogma of faith in 1950: "We pronounce, declare and define it to be a divinely revealed dogma that the immaculate Mother of God, the ever Virgin Mary, having completed the course of her earthly life, was assumed body and soul to heavenly glory." *Defining the Dogma of the Assumption, Munificentissimus Deus, Apostolic Constitution of Pope Pius XII issued November 1, 1950*

Catechism of the Catholic Church (CCC) #966: "'Finally the Immaculate Virgin, preserved free from all stain of original sin, when the course of her earthly life was finished, was taken up body and soul into heavenly glory, and exalted by the Lord as Queen over all things, so that she might be the more fully conformed to her Son, the Lord of lords and conqueror of sin and death.'[1] The Assumption of the Blessed Virgin is a singular participation in her Son's Resurrection and an anticipation of the resurrection of other Christians." [1]*LG* 59; cf. Pius XII, *Munificentissimus Deus* (1950): DS 3903; cf. *Rev* 19:16.

"Just as the Mother of Jesus, glorified in body and soul in heaven, is the image and beginning of the Church as it is to be perfected in the world to come, so too does she shine forth on earth, until the day of the Lord shall come, (cf. 2 Pet. 3:10) as a sign of sure hope and solace to the people of God during its sojourn on earth." *From Vatican II, Dogmatic Constitution on the Church, (68) 75*

1 Corinthians 15:13-18 [13] But if there is no resurrection of the dead, then Christ has not been raised; [14] if Christ has not been raised, then our preaching is in vain and your faith is in vain. [15] We are even found to be misrepresenting God, because we testified of God that he raised Christ, whom he did not raise if it is true that the dead are not raised. [16] For if the dead are not raised, then Christ has not been raised. [17] If Christ has not been raised, your faith is futile and you are still in your sins. [18] Then those also who have fallen asleep in Christ have perished.

Reflection: The Bible and the Catholic Church teach that we are to worship God alone and to love God above all things. We follow Mary's example if we love and worship Jesus as our Lord and Savior. Do you love and worship Jesus like Mary did?

After her death and entrance into heaven, Mary was crowned Queen of Heaven. She is a Queen because she is the mother of Jesus, who is called King because he is our Savior and the Son of God. She is not only Queen, but also our spiritual mother in heaven who loves us very much and intercedes for us with her Son Jesus. We should love and honor Mary just as Jesus loves and honors her.

Luke 1:46-49 [46]And Mary said, "My soul magnifies the Lord, [47]and my spirit rejoices in God my Savior, [48]for he has regarded the low estate of his handmaiden. For behold, henceforth all generations will call me blessed; [49]for he who is mighty has done great things for me, and holy is his name."

The Coronation of the Virgin
by Diego Velázquez, 1641-1644

Ad Caeli Reginam: Encyclical of Pope Pius XII Proclaiming the Queenship of Mary
"From the earliest ages of the catholic church a Christian people . . . has addressed prayers of petition and hymns of praise and veneration to the Queen of heaven. And never has that hope wavered which they placed in the Mother of the Divine King, Jesus Christ; nor has that faith ever failed by which we are taught that Mary, the Virgin Mother of God, reigns with a mother's solicitude over the entire world, just as she is crowned in heavenly blessedness with the glory of a Queen…. 38. From these considerations, the proof develops on these lines: if Mary, in taking an active part in the work of salvation, was, by God's design, associated with Jesus Christ, the source of salvation itself, in a manner comparable to that in which Eve was associated with Adam, the source of death, so that it may be stated that the work of our salvation was accomplished by a kind of 'recapitulation,' in which a virgin was instrumental in the salvation of the human race, just as a virgin had been closely associated with its death; if, moreover, it can likewise be stated that this glorious Lady had been chosen Mother of Christ 'in order that she might become a partner in the redemption of the human race'; and if, in truth, 'it was she who, free of the stain of actual and original sin, and ever most closely bound to her Son, on Golgotha offered that Son to the Eternal Father together with the complete sacrifice of her maternal rights and maternal love, like a new Eve, for all the sons of Adam, stained as they were by his lamentable fall,' then it may be legitimately concluded that as Christ, the new Adam, must be called a King not merely because He is Son of God, but also because He is our Redeemer, so, analogously, the Most Blessed Virgin is queen not only because she is Mother of God, but also because, as the new Eve, she was associated with the new Adam."

> **Reflection:** Mary's example shows us how to worship, love, and follow Jesus; Jesus shows us how to love and honor Mary. Do you love and honor Mary as Jesus did?

An Overview of God's Revelation

God exists and reveals himself to us. "God, infinitely perfect and blessed in himself, in a plan of sheer goodness freely created man to make him share in his own blessed life. For this reason, at every time and in every place, God draws close to man. He calls man to seek him, to know him, to love him with all his strength. He calls together all men, scattered and divided by sin, into the unity of his family, the Church. To accomplish this, when the fullness of time had come, God sent his Son as Redeemer and Saviour. In his Son and through him, he invites men to become, in the Holy Spirit, his adopted children and thus heirs of his blessed life" (*CCC* #1).

There are many reasons to believe in God's existence from reason, creation, and verified miracles, but faith is a gift from God that we can choose to accept or reject. We have free will to decide if we will search for, believe in, and follow God. Chances are, if we do not seek God and his plan for us, we will not find them, even if we learn all the reasons and science supporting the miracles performed throughout the ages.

To learn about God, we should study the Bible, official Church teachings (vatican.va), and writings of the Saints. To know experientially that God exists, we should pray and do what God asks of us. The more we seek and pray and do what God asks, the more we will experience God and know that what he says is true. "Ask, and it will be given you; seek, and you will find; knock, and it will be opened to you" (Matthew 7:7).

God loves us as his children and made us for union with himself. There is nothing greater than God that can ultimately fulfill us. God created us out of love and for love. It is like we have a God-shaped hole in our hearts that only God can fill.

The Old Testament: Our Jewish Roots

To understand God and the teachings of his only begotten Son Jesus Christ, it helps to be familiar with the Old Testament of the Bible. The Old Testament is a history of God's work from creation to the time of Jesus Christ. Below is a short summary.

In Genesis, the first book of the Bible, God created the universe and all that is in it including Adam and Eve, the first man and woman, from whom all other humans have descended. God put them in a beautiful garden called Paradise where there was no sickness, sin, or death. He told them not to eat the fruit of one tree in the garden.

Before God made humans, he made the angels, giving both free will. Some angels due to their pride rejected God and were dispelled from heaven. These fallen angels are referred to as devils or demons. They want humans to reject God also. One fallen angel, Satan, (disguised as a serpent) tempted Eve to disobey God. She listened and ate the forbidden fruit and gave some to Adam to eat, and he disobeyed God also.

This is called Original Sin because it was the first human sin. (Sin means we freely choose to do something we know is wrong and against God's will, or not to do something we can do that we know we should do.) When sin is about a grave matter, we can lose God's grace (God's life) in our soul that we received at baptism. This is called a serious or mortal sin. But God forgives us if we are truly sorry and repent. If we truly love God, we will do what God wants us to do. God is all good. He created us and loves us. He wants us to love him in return so we can be happy now and forever.

"And we have seen and testify that the Father has sent his Son as the Savior of the world. Whoever confesses that Jesus is the Son of God, God abides in him, and he in God. So we know and believe the love God has for us. God is love, and he who abides in love abides in God, and God abides in him" (1 John 4:14-16).

God knows all things, is all powerful, and wanted what was best for Adam and Eve, but Adam and Eve thought they knew more than God regarding what was best for them and disobeyed God. The result of their sin was that they had to leave Paradise and were subject to sickness and death. They lost other gifts for themselves and also for us, their descendants, and we have inherited the effects of their sin. "As a result of original sin, human nature is weakened in its powers, subject to ignorance, suffering and the domination of death, and inclined to sin…" (*CCC* #418).

God created the world, and it was good, but through sin, evil entered the world. The good news is that God promised Adam and Eve that he would send a Savior to save the world from sin and to reopen the gates of heaven that were closed by Adam and Eve's sin. This Savior is called the Messiah and is Jesus Christ.

Over time, Adam and Eve had many descendants until there were many people in the world. God made a covenant with some of their descendants who came to be known as the Chosen People, Israelites, or Jewish people. God sent prophets to teach them and to prepare them for the coming of the promised Messiah.

New Testament: Our Savior Jesus Christ

Jesus Christ is the long-awaited Messiah and Savior of the world. He is God the Son, the second person of the Trinity (Father, Son, and Holy Spirit), who became also a human being through being born of Mary. "For God so loved the world that he gave his only Son, that whoever believes in him should not perish but have eternal life" (John 3:16). The New Testament records what Jesus really did and taught.

Before Jesus rose into heaven he founded his Church. "And I tell you, you are Peter, and on this rock I will build my church, and the powers of death shall not prevail against it" (Matthew 16:18). The Nicene Creed summarizes Christ's teachings handed down from the apostles in his Church, "We believe in one God, the Father, the Almighty, Maker of heaven and earth, of all that is seen and unseen. We believe in one Lord Jesus Christ, the only Son of God, eternally begotten of the Father; God from God, Light from Light, true God from true God; begotten not made, one in being with the Father. Through Him all things were made. For us men and for our salvation He came down from heaven. By the power of the Holy Spirit He was born of the Virgin Mary and became man. For our sake He was crucified under Pontius Pilate. He suffered, died, and was buried. On the third day he rose again, in fulfillment of the Scriptures. He ascended into heaven and is seated at the right hand of the Father. He will come again in glory to judge the living and the dead, and his kingdom will have no end. We believe in the Holy Spirit, the Lord, the Giver of life, who proceeds from the Father and the Son. With the Father and the Son he is worshipped and glorified. He has spoken through the Prophets. We believe in one holy catholic and apostolic Church. We acknowledge one baptism for the forgiveness of sins. We look for the resurrection of the dead, and the life of the world to come. Amen." (from the Vatican website at www.vatican.va/archive/ccc_css/archive/catechism/credo.htm)

The Fatima Story

The Blessed Virgin Mary has appeared many times to various people in history, and one outstanding appearance was at Fatima, Portugal. Our Lady of Fatima appeared to three children, Lucia dos Santos and her cousins, Jacinta and Francisco Marto, in Fatima for six consecutive months starting on May 13, 1917. Mary told the children many things including to pray the rosary daily to obtain peace in the world and to offer sacrifices for the conversion of sinners. Mary also predicted future events that came true and gave the children three secrets, which they could tell later.

Our Lady of Fatima

Apparitions of the Angel in 1916

Before the Blessed Mother appeared to the children at Fatima, an angel appeared to them three times in 1916.

The first time they were tending their sheep and a strong wind shook the trees. Startled, the children looked up to see a figure coming towards them above the trees. Lucia said, "It was a young man, about fourteen or fifteen years old, whiter than snow, transparent as crystal when the sun shines through it, and of great beauty. On reaching us, he said: 'Do not be afraid! I am the Angel of Peace. Pray with me.' Kneeling on the ground, he bowed down until his forehead touched the ground, and made us repeat these words three times: 'My God, I believe, I adore, I hope and I love You! I ask pardon of You for those who do not believe, do not adore, do not hope and do not love You.'"*

At the second appearance the Angel said, "Pray, pray very much! The most holy Hearts of Jesus and Mary have designs of mercy on you. Offer prayers and sacrifices constantly to the Most High.... Make of everything you can a sacrifice, and offer it to God as an act of reparation for the sins by which He is offended, and in supplication for the conversion of sinners. You will thus draw down peace upon your country. I am its Angel Guardian, the Angel of Portugal. Above all, accept and bear with submission, the suffering which the Lord will send you."*

Another time while tending their sheep the Angel appeared again. Lucia said the Angel was "holding a chalice in his left hand, with the Host suspended above it, from which some drops of blood fell into the chalice.... The Angel knelt down beside us and made us repeat three times: 'Most Holy Trinity, Father, Son and Holy Spirit, I adore You profoundly, and I offer You the most precious Body, Blood, Soul and Divinity of Jesus Christ, present in all the tabernacles of the world, in reparation for the outrages, sacrileges and indifference with which He Himself is offended. And, through the infinite merits of His most Sacred Heart, and the Immaculate Heart of Mary, I beg of You the conversion of poor sinners.'"*

30

Apparitions of Mary in 1917

On May 13, 1917, ten-year-old Lucia and her younger cousins Jacinta and Francisco were tending sheep at the Cova da Iria near their home village of Fatima, Portugal. Lucia saw a woman "more brilliant than the sun, and radiated a light more clear and intense than a crystal glass filled with sparkling water, when the rays of the burning sun shine through it."* Mary asked the children to do penance and "acts of reparation, and to make sacrifices to save sinners." (Sinners are people who through their own free choice disobey God by doing what they know is wrong, or by not doing what something they know they should do.) The conversion of sinners means to amend or change one's life according to the teachings of Jesus. Mary told the children that more souls go to hell for unrepented sins of impurity than for any other reason. She also said that certain styles and fashions were being introduced which gravely offend Jesus. This means we need to dress modestly so as not to be the occasion of sin to others. She told them other things as well.

The Blessed Mother also said to the children, "Sacrifice yourselves for sinners, and say many times to Jesus, especially whenever you make some sacrifice: O Jesus, it is for love of You, for the conversion of sinners, and in reparation for the sins committed against the Immaculate Heart of Mary."*

> **Our Lady of Fatima said, "Pray the Rosary every day, in order to obtain peace for the world and the end of the war."**

The seers of Fatima: Lúcia Santos (left) with her cousins, Francisco and Jacinta Marto, in 1917

On one occasion, Lucia asked Mary if she would take them to heaven. Mary said, "Yes. I will take Jacinta and Francisco soon. But you are to stay here some time longer. Jesus wishes to make use of you to make me known and loved. He wants to establish in the world devotion to my Immaculate Heart."* This prophecy later came true as both Francisco and Jacinta died from complications from the Spanish flu while still children, but Lucia became a nun and lived to be 97 years old.

When people heard about the visions and miracles at Fatima, thousands of people came to see for themselves. On August 13, 1917, the government administrator, who didn't believe in the Catholic religion and did not like crowds coming to Fatima, put the children in jail. The administrator questioned the children and tried to get them to tell the secrets Mary had told them not to tell yet. The children refused even though he said he would boil them in oil if they did not tell him the secrets. The children were aged 10, 9, and 7 at the time.

The Miracle of the Sun

Mary promised a miracle would occur in October so that all may believe. About 70,000 people came that day to see what would happen including newspaper reporters and photographers.

All of a sudden, Lucia called out to the crowd to look at the sun. Thousands of people including some atheists saw the sun appearing to change colors and rotate

The crowd watching the miracle of the "Dance of the Sun" at Fatima, October 13, 1917

like a wheel. Some people watching thought the sun was falling to the earth. Some thought it was the end of the world. Even some people in nearby towns saw the miracle.

Reports of the Miracle of the Sun

O Século (a pro-government, anti-clerical, Lisbon newspaper), reported the following: "Before the astonished eyes of the crowd, whose aspect was biblical as they stood bareheaded, eagerly searching the sky, the sun trembled, made sudden incredible movements outside all cosmic laws---the sun "danced" according to the typical expression of the people."

An eye witness quoted in the newspaper *Ordem* said, "The sun, at one moment surrounded with scarlet flame, at another aureoled in yellow and deep purple, seemed to be in an exceedingly fast and whirling movement, at times appearing to be loosened from the sky and to be approaching the earth, strongly radiating heat."

The October 17, 1917 edition of the Lisbon Daily, *O Dia,* reported the following, "At one o'clock in the afternoon, midday by the sun, the rain stopped. The sky, pearly grey in colour, illuminated the vast arid landscape with a strange light. The sun had a transparent gauzy veil so that the eyes could easily be fixed upon it. The grey mother-of-pearl tone turned into a sheet of silver which broke up as the clouds were torn apart and the silver sun, enveloped in the same gauzy grey light, was seen to whirl and turn in the circle of broken clouds. A cry went up from every mouth and people fell on their knees on the muddy ground.... The light turned a beautiful blue, as if it had come through the stained-glass windows of a cathedral, and spread itself over the people who knelt with outstretched hands. The blue faded slowly, and then the light seemed to pass through yellow glass. Yellow stains fell against white hand-kerchiefs, against the dark skirts of the women. They were repeated on the trees, on the stones and on the serra. People wept and prayed with uncovered heads, in the presence of a miracle they had awaited. The seconds seemed like hours, so vivid were they."
(The above quotes on the miracle are a few of many reported at www.ewtn.com/fatima.)

Sr. Lucia of Fatima on Penance: "Many persons feeling that the word penance implies great austerities, and not feeling that they have the strength for great sacrifices, become discouraged and continue a life of lukewarmness and sin." Then she said Our Lord explained: "The sacrifice required of every person is the fulfillment of one's duties in life and the observance of My law. This is the penance that I now seek and require" (www.rosary-center.org/fatimams.html).

The Secret of Fatima (Three Parts)

The first part of the secret was a vision of hell, which Lucia describes as follows: "Our Lady showed us a great sea of fire which seemed to be under the earth. Plunged in this fire were demons and souls in human form, like transparent burning embers, all blackened or burnished bronze, floating about in the conflagration, now raised into the air by the flames that issued from within themselves together with great clouds of smoke, now falling back on every side like sparks in a huge fire, without weight or equilibrium, and amid shrieks and groans of pain and despair, which horrified us and made us tremble with fear. The demons could be distinguished by their terrifying and repulsive likeness to frightful and unknown animals, all black and transparent. This vision lasted but an instant. How can we ever be grateful enough to our kind heavenly Mother, who had already prepared us by promising, in the first Apparition, to take us to heaven? Otherwise, I think we would have died of fear and terror."*

The second part of the secret included Mary's instructions on how to help save souls from hell. Lucia's Third Memoir said: "We then looked up at Our Lady, who said to us so kindly and so sadly: "You have seen hell where the souls of poor sinners go. To save them, God wishes to establish in the world devotion to my Immaculate Heart. If what I say to you is done, many souls will be saved and there will be peace. The war is going to end: but if people do not cease offending God, a worse one will break out during the Pontificate of Pius XI. When you see a night illumined by an unknown light, know that this is the great sign given you by God that he is about to punish the world for its crimes, by means of war, famine, and persecutions of the Church and of the Holy Father. To prevent this, I shall come to ask for the consecration of Russia to my Immaculate Heart, and the Communion of reparation on the First Saturdays. If my requests are heeded, Russia will be converted, and there will be peace; if not, she will spread her errors throughout the world, causing wars and persecutions of the Church. The good will be martyred; the Holy Father will have much to suffer; various nations will be annihilated. In the end, my Immaculate Heart will triumph. The Holy Father will consecrate Russia to me, and she shall be converted, and a period of peace will be granted to the world."*

This all happened as Mary said it would as people did not do what was needed. In Russia the Communists took over. They killed millions of people and took over other countries and spread the errors of Communism. They took away many freedoms such as the freedom of religion and speech, and sometimes personal property.

"The third part of the secret revealed at the Cova da Iria-Fatima, on 13 July 1917…. After the two parts which I have already explained, at the left of Our Lady and a little above, we saw an Angel with a flaming sword in his left hand; flashing, it gave out flames that looked as though they would set the world on fire; but they died out in contact with the splendor that Our Lady radiated towards him from her right hand: pointing to the earth with his right hand, the Angel cried out in a loud voice: 'Penance, Penance, Penance!' And we saw in an immense light that is God: 'something similar to how people appear in a mirror when they pass in front of it' a Bishop dressed in White 'we had the impression that it was the Holy Father'. Other Bishops, Priests, men and women Religious going up a steep mountain, at the top of which there was a big Cross of rough-hewn trunks as of a cork-tree with the bark; before reaching there the Holy Father passed through a big city half in ruins and half trembling with halting step, afflicted with pain and sorrow, he prayed for the souls of the corpses he met on his way; having reached the top of the mountain, on his knees at the foot of the big Cross he was killed by a group of soldiers who fired bullets and arrows at him, and in the same way there died one after another the other Bishops, Priests, men and women Religious, and various lay people of different ranks and positions. Beneath the two arms of the Cross there were two Angels each with a crystal aspersorium in his hand, in which they gathered up the blood of the Martyrs and with it sprinkled the souls that were making their way to God. - *Tuy-3-1-1944*"*

*Quotes from *Fatima in Lucia's Own Words*, www.catholic-soe-org/catholicbooks.html.

Official Position of the Church

Private revelations are not part of the Catholic Church's "deposit of faith", and there is not a requirement for Catholics to believe them; however, the Church studied the Fatima apparitions and called them "worthy of belief." Also the Church canonized Jacinta and Francisco as Saints, and Lucia's life is being studied for canonization. Jacinta, who died at age 10, is possibly the youngest non-martyred canonized saint.

Fatima: Reaffirmation of the Gospel

The Fatima message and the associated miracles reaffirm many teachings of the Catholic faith such as the fact that God exists and is involved in our world, the Gospel messages of Jesus, prayer, sin, heaven, hell, angels, miracles, and the Eucharist as the body, blood, soul and divinity of Jesus Christ. It also encourages devotion to Mary.

Ideas for Praying the Family Rosary with Children

Choose a time to pray that works for the family so that prayer becomes a regular part of daily life. A time to pray the rosary could be right before the children's bedtime. Before starting prayer, perhaps turn the lights down low and allow the children to take turns lighting a special candle and blowing it out afterwards. When they see the lights off, the candle burning, and everyone else praying, they may want to be included. Another idea is for the children to take turns leading the prayers for one decade and invite them to add their own intentions before beginning. Children and teens often have serious concerns. Saying the rosary for their intentions may help them feel included. It's a good idea for each child to have a rosary to use. Making their own special rosary is a possibility. If saying the entire rosary is too difficult for the children, perhaps excuse them after one decade. Be sure to announce the mystery for each decade and maybe explain it a little. When teaching them about their Catholic faith, include stories about approved Marian apparitions like Fatima, so they will better understand the reasons to pray the rosary. The goal is to learn to love Jesus and Mary, to encourage them to pray, and to associate prayer with a positive experience.

> "There is no surer means of calling down God's blessings upon the family . . . than the daily recitation of the Rosary." ~ *Pope Pius XII*

Fifteen Promises of the Blessed Virgin to Christians Who Faithfully Pray the Rosary

Our Lady gave these to St. Dominic and to the Dominican Blessed Alan de la Roche.

1. To all those who shall pray my Rosary devoutly, I promise my special protection and great graces.
2. Those who shall persevere in the recitation of my Rosary will receive some special grace.
3. The Rosary will be a very powerful armor against hell; it will destroy vice, deliver from sin and dispel heresy.
4. The rosary will make virtue and good works flourish, and will obtain for souls the most abundant divine mercies. It will draw the hearts of men from the love of the world and its vanities, and will lift them to the desire of eternal things. Oh, that souls would sanctify themselves by this means.
5. Those who trust themselves to me through the Rosary will not perish.
6. Whoever recites my Rosary devoutly reflecting on the mysteries, shall never be overwhelmed by misfortune. He will not experience the anger of God nor will he perish by an unprovided death. The sinner will be converted; the just will persevere in grace and merit eternal life.
7. Those truly devoted to my Rosary shall not die without the sacraments of the Church.
8. Those who are faithful to recite my Rosary shall have during their life and at their death the light of God and the plenitude of His graces and will share in the merits of the blessed.
9. I will deliver promptly from purgatory souls devoted to my Rosary.
10. True children of my Rosary will enjoy great glory in heaven.
11. What you shall ask through my Rosary you shall obtain.
12. To those who propagate my Rosary I promise aid in all their necessities.
13. I have obtained from my Son that all the members of the Rosary Confraternity shall have as their intercessors, in life and in death, the entire celestial court.
14. Those who recite my Rosary faithfully are my beloved children, the brothers and sisters of Jesus Christ.
15. Devotion to my Rosary is a special sign of predestination.

(The promises listed are from www.rosary-center.org/conprom.htm)

> "The Rosary basically was given to St Dominic to overcome heresy and to promote virtue." "That's why in approved apparitions of the Church, Our Lady talks about the Rosary, tells us pray the Rosary…at Fatima she talked about the importance the Rosary as our weapon against vice, sin, and falsehood." ~*Fr. Donald Calloway*

> "The holy Rosary is a powerful weapon. Use it with confidence and you'll be amazed at the results." ~ *St. Josemaria Escriva*

Made in United States
Troutdale, OR
07/02/2023